Class Trip
PHILADELPHIA

Russell Roberts

Mitchell Lane
PUBLISHERS

Franklin Library
Summit Public Schools

P.O. Box 196
Hockessin, Delaware 19707
Visit us on the web: www.mitchelllane.com
Comments? email us: mitchelllane@mitchelllane.com

Mitchell Lane
PUBLISHERS

Boston • New York
Philadelphia • San Antonio
San Diego • Washington, D.C.

Printing   1   2   3   4   5   6   7   8   9

Library of Congress Cataloging-in-Publication Data

Roberts, Russell, 1953–
 Class trip Philadelphia / by Russell Roberts.
   p. cm.—(Robbie reader, class trip)
 Includes bibliographical references and index.
 ISBN 978-1-58415-807-3 (library bound)
 1. Philadelphia (Pa.)—Juvenile literature. 2. Philadelphia (Pa.)—History—Juvenile literature.
 I. Title.
 F158.33.R63 2010
 974.8'11—dc22
                                    2009001106

                                    PLB

CONTENTS

PHILADELPHIA

At nearly 548 feet high, Philadelphia's City Hall is the tallest masonry building in the world. At its peak is a bronze statue of William Penn. Right: Cole Hamels of the Phillies

Field Trip

I was sitting in my fourth-period social studies class, just thinking about what a nice warm spring day it was outside, when in walked Ms. Reynolds, our teacher. She was carrying a large stack of newspapers. On top of the pile was her purse. The pile was so high that her purse was almost up to her chin!

"Brian Rasoldi," she said, calling my name. "Please go out to the hall and bring in the rest of the things I have out there." She dropped the pile of papers onto her desk with a plop.

"Sure," I said. I hopped out of my chair and went out to the hall. Sitting on the floor next to the door was a small green stuffed doll wearing a Philadelphia Phillies shirt. There was also a copy of the Declaration of Independence. It was in a glass frame, like a picture. I also found a library book, a red fireman's hat, and an empty paper plate.

I brought those things into the classroom and placed them on Ms. Reynolds' desk. She was across the room, opening a window.

"Thank you, Brian," she said. Then she walked back to her desk and carefully arranged all the objects—the pile of newspapers, the green doll, the Declaration of Independence, the library book, the fireman's hat, and the paper plate. Then she looked at us.

"Now, my fourth-grade social studies class," she said, smiling, "what do all these things have in common?"

I stared at the objects, as did everybody else. But nobody had an answer. Through the open window I could hear a bird chirping.

"Come on, boys and girls," Ms. Reynolds said. "Do you mean to tell me that my smart students in Bordentown's Thomas Paine Elementary School can't figure this out?" She smiled again, and brushed her reddish hair from her forehead.

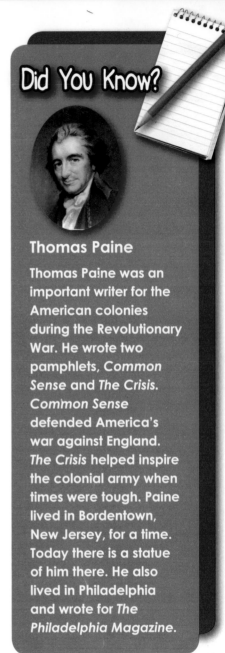

Did You Know?

Thomas Paine

Thomas Paine was an important writer for the American colonies during the Revolutionary War. He wrote two pamphlets, *Common Sense* and *The Crisis*. *Common Sense* defended America's war against England. *The Crisis* helped inspire the colonial army when times were tough. Paine lived in Bordentown, New Jersey, for a time. Today there is a statue of him there. He also lived in Philadelphia and wrote for *The Philadelphia Magazine*.

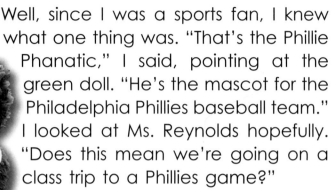

Well, since I was a sports fan, I knew what one thing was. "That's the Phillie Phanatic," I said, pointing at the green doll. "He's the mascot for the Philadelphia Phillies baseball team." I looked at Ms. Reynolds hopefully. "Does this mean we're going on a class trip to a Phillies game?"

"No," she said, laughing. "But you're close, Brian. We're going on a class trip to the city of Philadelphia!"

Everybody started talking excitedly. Class trips were great!

"All right, class, quiet down," said Ms. Reynolds. "Over the next week we'll be studying all about Philadelphia. Then we'll take a bus trip there to see some of the city's most famous sites."

Nadine raised her hand. "Are you going to tell us what those objects on your desk have to do with Philadelphia, Ms. Reynolds?" she asked.

"In a minute," answered the teacher. She pulled down a map of the United States that was rolled up in a green tube over the blackboard. The fifty states were in different colors, and some cities were named in each state.

"All right," she said. "Here we are in New Jersey." She pointed to a state right next to the Atlantic Ocean. "That's on the East Coast. Does anybody know where Philadelphia, Pennsylvania, is?"

My friend Buttons raised his hand and went up to the blackboard. His real name was Alex, but we called him Buttons because he always seemed to lose buttons from his shirt, and then we'd have to look for them. He pointed to the state of Pennsylvania. It was right next to New Jersey.

Next, Ms. Reynolds pulled down a map that showed only Pennsylvania and had Buttons find Philadelphia. It is in southeastern Pennsylvania, a little bit south of where we were in Bordentown, which is near Trenton.

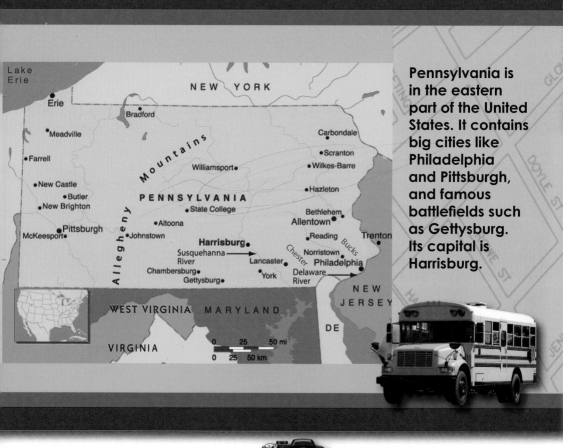

Pennsylvania is in the eastern part of the United States. It contains big cities like Philadelphia and Pittsburgh, and famous battlefields such as Gettysburg. Its capital is Harrisburg.

The Declaration of Independence was signed on a hot summer's day in Philadelphia in 1776. In a bold move by the Congress, it declared the American colonies free and independent of England, which was then the most powerful nation in the world.

New Jersey and Pennsylvania are separated by a river called the Delaware. Both Bordentown and Philadelphia are right next to the Delaware River.

"That's right," said Ms. Reynolds. "Indeed, the Delaware River has played an important part in Philadelphia's becoming one of the ten largest cities in the United States.

"And now," she continued, "about these objects on my desk." She pointed to them. "The copy of the Declaration is here because the original Declaration

The Declaration of Independence

Pennsylvania

1 Franklin Institute
2 City Hall
3 Pennsylvania Convention Center
4 Pat's Steaks
5 Mummers Museum
6 Citizens Bank Park
7 Fort Mifflin
8 U.S. Mint
9 Christ Church
10 Constitution Center
11 Betsy Ross House
12 Atwater Kent Museum
13 Independence Hall

of Independence was written in Philadelphia. The newspapers are copies of the *Philadelphia Inquirer.* You can learn a lot about a city by reading one of its newspapers, so everyone in class is going to get one. The library book and fireman's hat have to do with Benjamin Franklin. He was one of Philadelphia's most famous citizens. He helped start the city's first library and fire department.

Fireman's hat

Philly cheese steak

"And finally," she said, laughing, "the paper plate is for a Philadelphia cheese steak . . . one of the city's most famous foods, as well as one of my favorite meals. Now for homework, I need everyone to find out all you can about Philadelphia."

I looked at Buttons and he smiled. This meant only one thing: study group!

Scouts from William Penn's expedition landed in what is now Philadelphia Right: Charles II of England

Study Group

Study groups were my favorite way to do homework. Buttons, Raj Patel, Mary Shelley, Jim Nitka, Tanisha Brown, and I would get together in the Bordentown Library after school to work on homework assignments. We'd share the information we found, so we'd get a lot done fast. This assignment on Philadelphia was perfect for our study group, so later that day the six of us met in the library and started hitting the books and the Internet. Pretty soon, we had found out a lot.

"Philadelphia is one of America's most historical cities," Buttons said. "It was founded by William Penn in 1682. One year earlier, Penn received a royal grant from Charles II of England, giving Penn the colony of Pennsylvania. Penn said that he would establish 'a large Towne or Citty in the most convenient place upon the River for health & Navigation.' "

"I found that, too," said Raj. "Penn sent three men to find land for his new city. They bought an undeveloped piece of land from three Swedish men and began to plan the city, which was called

Did You Know?

William Penn was the founder of Pennsylvania and designer of Philadelphia. He was born in London, England, in 1644. He was a Quaker, and his religion was not popular in England. In 1681, King Charles granted Penn some land in the New World so that he could practice his religion there. This land became the state of Pennsylvania ("Penn's Woods"). Penn did not spend much time in Pennsylvania because troubles in England constantly forced him to return there. He died in 1718.

Philadelphia. The word *Philadelphia* is Greek, and means 'City of Brotherly Love.' "

"What were Swedish guys doing there?" I asked.

"Well," said Raj, "it says here that the Swedish, English, and Dutch had been trying to settle along the Delaware River since 1609, when Henry Hudson explored the river for the Dutch. They all wanted to trade in fur."

"What about the Native Americans?" Jim asked.

Tanisha answered, "According to legend, Penn made a treaty of friendship with the Lenni Lenape [LEH-nee len-NAH-pay] tribe in 1683. They met under a large elm tree in the village of Shackamaxon, in what is now the Kensington area of Philadelphia. Penn wanted the city to be peaceful, and he didn't want to have to build walls to protect it from attack."

"Before that," said Raj, "when Penn first arrived here from England, he thought that the way his new city was being laid out was too cramped. He wanted a 'greene Country Towne.' So he expanded it to the west, to the Schuylkill River, and set about redesigning the city. He drew it with at least 800 feet between

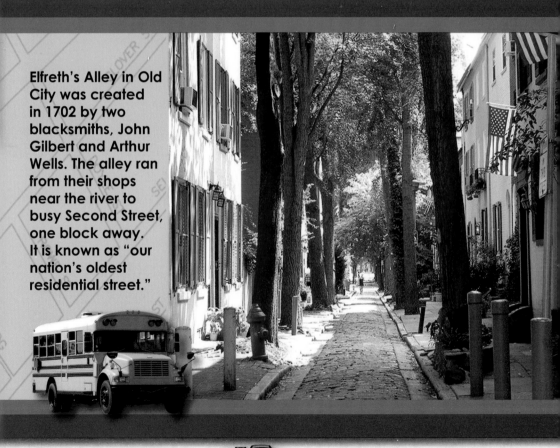

Elfreth's Alley in Old City was created in 1702 by two blacksmiths, John Gilbert and Arthur Wells. The alley ran from their shops near the river to busy Second Street, one block away. It is known as "our nation's oldest residential street."

Reenactors at Fort Mifflin, the site of a Revolutionary War battle. In 1777, the British Army attacked the fort. The American soldiers held out long enough to allow George Washington and his weary army to escape to Valley Forge for the winter.

each house, and that space was to be planted with gardens and **orchards**. He wanted Philadelphia to be a city of country gentlemen."

"But it didn't turn out like that," I added. "Some of the first residents lived in caves along the riverbank. Instead of expanding to the Schuylkill, the early settlers bought lots along the Delaware River, then divided them into even smaller lots. So his uncrowded city became very cramped."

"People of different religions, such as Catholics, Jews, and Quakers, heard that Philadelphia was a place where everyone could live in peace, so they started moving in, too," added Jim. "By 1701, the city had around 2,500 people, and it just kept growing. Because it was on the Delaware River, it also became a major port."

"Philadelphia was the capital of the Pennsylvania colony, and in 1732 the city began building a new state house at Fifth and Sixth streets," I said. "Today it's called Independence Hall."

"That's what I found, too," said Tanisha. I think she had a crush on Jim, because she kept looking at him. "By the 1760s, Philadelphia was one of the major cities of the thirteen American colonies, along with Boston and New York. Philadelphia is where the **delegates** to

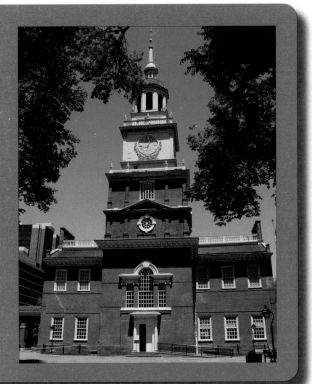

It took over twenty years to construct Independence Hall, which was initially intended to be the Pennsylvania State House. Both the Declaration of Independence and the U.S. Constitution were debated and signed there. The hall is the prime attraction in the Independence National Historical Park.

the first Continental Congress met in 1774. Delegates met again in the Pennsylvania State House in 1775, and they adopted the Declaration of Independence in 1776. During the American Revolution, the

Betsy Ross' 13-star flag

city was occupied by the British for a time. After the war, the Constitutional Convention met there in 1787 and drafted the U.S. Constitution."

Buttons added, "Philadelphia was the capital of the United States in the beginning, but then the federal government moved to Washington, D.C. Even the state government moved away to Lancaster in 1799. Philadelphia was still the largest city in America in 1800, with a population of about 41,000. Over the next

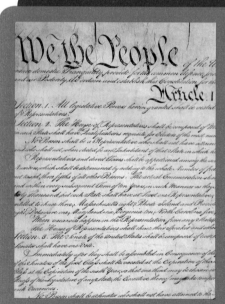

Did You Know?

The United States Constitution is the document by which America is governed. It was written by delegates at a special meeting held in Philadelphia in 1787. It replaced another document—the Articles of Confederation—that was first used by the United States after the Revolutionary War was over, but did not work well.

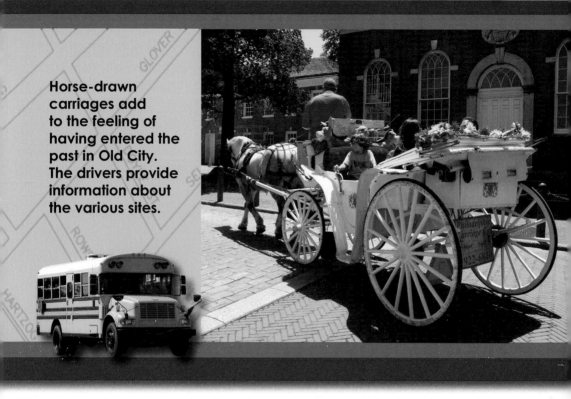

Horse-drawn carriages add to the feeling of having entered the past in Old City. The drivers provide information about the various sites.

hundred years, Philly became an industrial city, producing **textiles**, iron and steel, and sugar."

"In 1876, the **Centennial** Exposition, which was like a world's fair, was held in Philadelphia," said Raj, who was printing pages from the Internet. "New inventions like Alexander Graham Bell's telephone were displayed. Nine million people visited the exposition."

"That's when John Wanamaker opened his department store in an old Philadelphia railroad station," Mary chimed in. "It became one of the oldest department stores in the United States. Then, after about 1950, the same thing happened in Philadelphia that was going on in other Northern cities: factories and industries closed, the population shrank as people moved to the suburbs, and the city began to run out

Citizens Bank Park in Philadelphia is where the Philadelphia Phillies play Major League Baseball. It opened in 2004, and is one of the nicest of the "fan friendly" baseball stadiums that have been built in recent years.

Every year, the Philadelphia Auto Show is held to showcase new car models. The show is one of the largest in the United States.

of money. But by the end of that century, new life came to the city. It had a brand-new convention center, a baseball stadium that opened in 2004, and more tourists came to see the city's many historic places. In fact, in 2005, the magazine *National Geographic Traveler* named Philadelphia America's Next Great City because of its tourist attractions and renewal efforts."

By then our parents had come to pick us up and take us home. We agreed to meet at the library again the next day and learn more about Philadelphia.

PHILADELPHIA

Situated on the Delaware River, Philadelphia has become an important commercial and business center. It also offers fun activities such as dinner cruises and sailing. Right: Mummers

More About Philly

The next day, the six of us met again at the library and continued our Philadelphia project.

"Philadelphia has two major rivers: the Delaware and the Schuylkill [SKOO-kill]," said Raj. "The Delaware is the longest undammed river east of the Mississippi. It flows for 330 miles from lower New York state through Pennsylvania, New Jersey, and Delaware to the Atlantic Ocean. The Schuylkill is about 130 miles long, and it lies entirely in Pennsylvania."

Mary continued, "The area around the Delaware River, from Trenton, New Jersey, and south past Wilmington, Delaware, is called the Delaware Valley. More than five million people live in this area. Far to the west of the city are the Appalachian Mountains, and east, past New Jersey, is the Atlantic Ocean. Because Philadelphia lies between the mountains and the ocean, its climate isn't too cold or too hot—just like it is in Bordentown."

Tanisha piped up. "I found a few facts about Philly's climate on the Internet," she said. "Its elevation ranges from 5 feet all the way to 431 feet above sea level. Its average temperature is 53 degrees. It gets about 40 inches of rain per year, and over 20 inches of snow."

"Look at this," said Jim, holding up a heavy book. "Once the Philadelphia waterfront welcomed sailing ships from around the world, as merchants brought goods back and forth to it. Today, the area where William Penn is believed to have first landed is called Penn's Landing. It's a riverside park where concerts and festivals are held, and there's a ship museum there."

"My parents took me to the Philadelphia Museum of Art once," Buttons said. "It's one of the leading art museums in the country. A lot of people like to run up the ninety-seven front steps, just like Rocky Balboa did in the movie *Rocky*." He laughed. "I tried it, but only made it halfway. I also lost a shirt button."

Mary said, "Philadelphia has a lot of great museums, like the Franklin Institute. It's a science museum named after Benjamin Franklin. When it was founded in 1824, it was called the Franklin Institute of the State of Pennsylvania for the Promotion of the Mechanic Arts. Over the years, new technology has been exhibited

The Rocky Statue, Philadelphia Museum of Art

The Sky Bike at the Franklin Institute travels along a wire three stories above the main lobby. Other exhibits there include a model of the human heart that visitors can walk through, and a lab where they can experiment with static electricity.

there, like in 1934, when Philo Farnsworth gave the first public demonstration of electronic television."

"There's the National Constitution Center," said Jim, "which is the only museum in the country dedicated to the United States Constitution."

"It also has its own orchestra—the Philadelphia Orchestra," said Mary.

"And a zoo," I said. My big sister Tess worked there, so I knew something about it. "The Philadelphia Zoo was America's first zoo. It opened in 1874. It has more than 1,300 animals, and it's in Fairmount Park, which is the largest **landscaped** park in the world. It covers 8,500 acres."

"Don't forget the Mummers," added Raj. "Every New Year's Day, the Mummers parade down Market Street in their fancy costumes."

"I'd rather see the Phillies play," I said. "Philadelphia has a team in all the major sports: Besides the Phillies, it has the Eagles in football, the Flyers in hockey, and the 76ers in basketball. They also have the Philadelphia Soul in Arena Football, which is football played indoors. The team is partly owned by rock superstar Jon Bon Jovi—a New Jerseyan!"

"Here's a question," said Tanisha. "Who runs Philadelphia?"

"The mayor," said Raj. "Philadelphia has the mayor-council form of city government. This means that the mayor is in overall charge of the city, but the council represents various parts, or districts, of the city. There

Did You Know?

Tigers play at the Philadelphia Zoo, the oldest zoo in the United States. The American Civil War delayed the zoo's opening until 1874. The zoo is home to more than 1,300 animals, many of which are endangered.

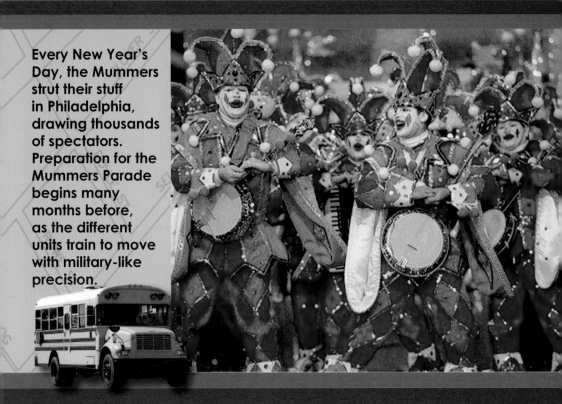

Every New Year's Day, the Mummers strut their stuff in Philadelphia, drawing thousands of spectators. Preparation for the Mummers Parade begins many months before, as the different units train to move with military-like precision.

are ten city council members. The mayor proposes laws, and the city council votes to approve or reject them."

By then my parents had come to pick us up. We all had pizza that night at my house. During dinner we agreed that we needed one more afternoon in the library to learn about Philadelphia. Ms. Reynolds wanted us to find out about famous Philadelphia citizens, including one who supposedly said, "All things considered, I'd rather be in Philadelphia"—and put it on his tombstone!

Now who could that be? No one knew.

Philadelphia native Joe Frazier (left) boxes Muhammad Ali for the Heavyweight Title in 1971. Right: Will Smith

Chapter

Famous Philadelphians

The next day we all met at the library for the last study group before our class trip to Philadelphia. We were looking for famous people from Philadelphia. Raj couldn't join us because he had flute practice with the school band. An hour after we met, the five of us had information about famous Philadelphians.

"We've talked before about William Penn," said Buttons. "Another famous person from Philly was Benjamin Franklin. He was an inventor, writer, printer, scientist, diplomat, and other things. He is one of the people most often associated with Philadelphia."

Mary said, "There was also Betsy Ross. According to legend, she sewed the first American flag that displayed the stars and stripes. The story might not be true, but most people believe it is."

"Marian Anderson, a famous African-American opera singer, also came from Philly," added Tanisha. "In 1939, she gave an open-air concert at the Lincoln Memorial in Washington, D.C., to an audience of 75,000 people. It was a national **sensation**!"

Chapter 4

Jim said, "A lot of actors lived in Philadelphia also. One of the most famous is Bill Cosby. There's also Will Smith, Kevin Bacon, and Richard Gere."

"A famous boxer named Joe Frazier is from Philly," I added. "In the 1970s he had several huge fights with heavyweight champ Muhammad Ali."

"Another actress from Philly was Grace Kelly," said Buttons. "She made some great movies with Alfred Hitchcock, like the creepy *Rear Window*. In 1956, she married Prince Rainier of the country of Monaco and became Princess Grace. Their wedding was spectacular."

"Speaking of spooky," said Mary, who likes to write scary stories, "don't forget M. Night Shyamalan. He's made all those creepy movies like *The Sixth Sense*."

"Don't forget Tina Fey of *30 Rock* and *Saturday Night Live*, and Larry from Moe, Larry, and Curly—the Three Stooges!" I said.

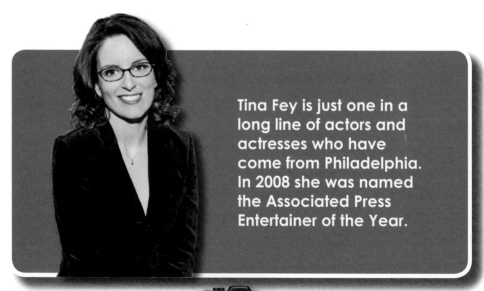

Tina Fey is just one in a long line of actors and actresses who have come from Philadelphia. In 2008 she was named the Associated Press Entertainer of the Year.

The Three Stooges: Larry, Curly, Moe

"I have someone that not a lot of people know about," said Buttons. "Margaret Mead was born in Philadelphia. She was a famous **anthropologist** who studied cultures and behaviors and lectured about them."

Buttons said, "There's also writer Louisa May Alcott. She wrote the famous novel *Little Women*. Other people from Philly are the singers Boyz II Men, hockey player Bobby Clarke, and George McClellan, who was a Union general during the Civil War."

"This is a great list," I said, "and there are plenty more people we could add to it. But did anybody find out who said 'All things considered, I'd rather be in Philadelphia'—and put it on his tombstone?"

No one had, and we were out of time. As I rode home with my sister Tess, I told her how we couldn't find that person.

Tess laughed. "That's W.C. Fields. He was a famous comedian from the early part of the twentieth century. The reason you couldn't find it is because the quote is written many different ways—and no one is even sure that he said it as he was dying! It might be just a legend."

That just proves that big sisters may be a pain sometimes, but they can be good for something!

Reenactors are ready to demonstrate colonial life. Thousands of students visit Philadelphia every year to walk in the footsteps of the Founding Fathers and hear stories about how they forged a new nation. Right: Benjamin Franklin

Chapter 5

Trip Day!

The day of our field trip to Philadelphia was bright and sunny—a perfect day! It seemed that even Mother Nature wanted us to have a good trip.

Our bus took us over the Delaware River from New Jersey into Philadelphia by way of the Benjamin Franklin Bridge. "There are also several other bridges that lead into the city at different places," said Ms. Reynolds. "There's the Betsy Ross Bridge, and also the Walt Whitman Bridge."

Once in the city, we headed for Independence National Historical Park. "The park spans over fifty-five acres on twenty city blocks," Ms. Reynolds said. "One of the buildings is Franklin Court, which is a museum built on the location of Benjamin Franklin's first permanent home in Philadelphia. Others include the National Constitution Center and the Independence Visitor Center. There's also the Atwater Kent Museum, which tells the story of Philadelphia. And of course, here is Independence Hall, where the United States of America was born."

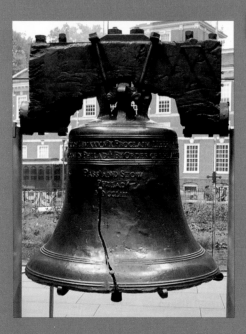

Did You Know?

The Liberty Bell was ordered in 1751 by the Pennsylvania Assembly. It was made in London, England, and shipped to Philadelphia. But the first time it was tested, it cracked. Although repairs were attempted over the years, the bell has not been rung since 1846 for fear of breaking it completely. It now can be seen in Liberty Bell Center near Independence Hall.

Although Independence Hall was considered large when it was first built, it looked small compared to the large office buildings across the street. But, as Ms. Reynolds reminded us, "very big things happened there." We got off the bus and followed a tour guide through the building, and she told us all about the signers of the Declaration of Independence. Then we walked past the Liberty Bell, and on through Old City toward the Delaware River.

"Philadelphia is a city of more than 100 neighborhoods," Ms. Reynolds said. "We won't have time to see everything in Old City, but later we'll drive past the Betsy Ross House. It has a flag with 13 stars hanging outside. Old City also contains the U.S. Mint, where coins are made. There's a small cemetery here called Christ Church Cemetery. This is where Benjamin Franklin was buried, along with his wife. There are also museums in Old City that deal with African-American history and American Jewish History."

After we'd walked just a few blocks, we reached Penn's Landing and the Independence Seaport Museum. There, we saw exhibits about how important

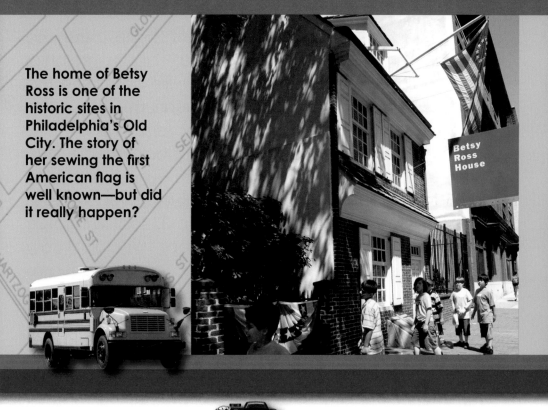

The home of Betsy Ross is one of the historic sites in Philadelphia's Old City. The story of her sewing the first American flag is well known—but did it really happen?

Betsy Ross House

The battleship *New Jersey* is docked on the waterfront in Camden, which is directly across the Delaware River from Philadelphia.

the Delaware and Schuylkill rivers have been to Philadelphia. We also learned all about colonial shipbuilding. Right across the water we could see the battleship *New Jersey* and an aquarium. They were on the waterfront in Camden, New Jersey.

After the seaport stop, we got back on the bus. We saw so many more things on our class trip to Philadelphia that it's hard to talk about everything. In Center City we saw City Hall. It has a 37-foot-tall statue of William Penn on the very top. We also saw Rittenhouse Square, one of the original squares designed by William Penn.

By then we were starving! We drove through South Philadelphia, past Citizens Bank Park where the Phillies play. We also passed the Mummers Museum. "Mumming began over two thousand years ago in

Europe and was brought to America by people coming to the New World," Ms. Reynolds explained.

"We read about the Mummers in the library," Mary said. "They dress up in all kinds of colorful costumes and dance, and some of them play music."

"I watched them on TV one year," said Buttons. "The parade lasted for hours. It was amazing how many people were in it."

"People have a lot of fun with mumming," said Ms. Reynolds. "And some take it very seriously. There's a

The Philadelphia Eagles are the city's National Football League team. Like the Phillies, the Eagles play in a fan-friendly stadium—Lincoln Financial Field, which opened in 2003.

big cash prize for the best acts, but the costumes can cost more than the prize money."

Finally we stopped at the Italian Market. It's indoors and outdoors, and people can buy all different types of cheeses, pasta, fruits, and vegetables. Near the market was a small restaurant with lots of outdoor tables. Ms. Reynolds ordered cheese steaks for everyone.

"The cheese steak is one of the foods that people all around the world associate with Philadelphia. So we're still studying the city," she said as a big gob of cheese dripped from her chin.

I don't know how many of us heard her. We were too busy eating. Best class trip ever!

Just The Facts

Founded: July 16, 1790

Location: Pennsylvania

Form of Government: Mayor

Land Area: 68.3 Square Miles

Population in 2007: about 1.5 million

U.S. Rank: The sixth most populous city in the U.S. (in 2007)

Highest Point: Chestnut Hill at 431 feet

Lowest Point: Sea level

Latitude: 39° 57' 8" N

Longitude: 75° 9' 51" W

Average Temperature: 55°F*

Hottest Day: July 20, 1930 & August 16, 1918 (106°F)

Coldest Day: February 11, 1899 (–15°F)

Average Annual Rainfall: About 40 inches

Major Industries: Manufacturing and distribution; service, information, engineering, and technology

Major Neighborhoods or Regions: Bridesburg, Center City, Chestnut Hill, Germantown, Kensington, Manayunk, Mount Airy, Northeast Philadelphia, Oak Lane, Old City, Olney, Penn's Landing, Richmond, Roxborough, South Philadelphia, Southwest Philadelphia, West Philly

Colleges and Universities: Art Institute of Philadelphia; Chestnut Hill College; Curtis Institute of Music; Drexel University; Holy Family University; La Salle University; Moore College of Art and Design; Pennsylvania Academy of the Fine Arts; Peirce College; Philadelphia University; Saint Joseph's University; Temple University; The Restaurant School at Walnut Hill College; Thomas Jefferson University; University of the Arts; University of Pennsylvania; University of the Sciences in Philadelphia

Public Parks: Fairmount Park, Washington Square Park, Roosevelt Park, Hunting Park, Fern Hill Park

Major Sports Teams: Phillies—Baseball; 76ers—Basketball; Flyers—Hockey; Eagles—Football

Major Museums and Cultural Centers: African American Museum in Philadelphia, Philadelphia Museum of Art, Franklin Institute, Kimmel Center, Mann Music Center, Mummers Museum, National Liberty Museum, National Museum of American Jewish History, Pennsylvania Academy of Fine Arts, Romanian Folk Art Museum, Rosenbach Museum and Library, Walnut Street Theatre, Woodmere Art Museum

*All weather statistics, U.S. National Weather Service, 2007

Make a Mummer's Mask

Mumming is an ancient custom that may go as far back as the early Romans. It began as a tradition around the New Year to drive away demons. Men and women would exchange clothes, wear masks, and then visit their neighbors' homes. There they would put on plays or other forms of entertainment. They would often receive food for their efforts. Philadelphians continue to celebrate the New Year with a Mummers parade that can last hours.

What You Need:
Thin cardboard
Pencil
Scissors
Elastic or ribbon
Feathers
Glue
Colored markers
Plastic gems (optional)

What You Do:

1   Cut your cardboard to make any shape you want. You might make a butterfly shape, or a flower, for example. You might also cut it so that it only covers your forehead.

2   Mark where your eyes will be and cut holes in those places.

3   Poke small holes near the sides of your mask. Thread one piece of ribbon through each hole. You will use the ribbon to tie your mask to your head.

4   Glue feathers to your mask. You can decorate part of your mask with colored markers and part of it with feathers, or you can cover all of the cardboard with feathers. Start near the center, and fan the feathers out as you go. You can also glue longer feathers to the inside of your mask, around the edges, with the fluffy tips sticking out. Glue on some plastic gems, too, if you want.

Philadelphia Historical Timeline

1682	William Penn founds Pennsylvania colony.
1701	William Penn grants a charter for the city of Philadelphia.
1706	The area now known as Washington Square is founded as a pauper's cemetery.
1723	Benjamin Franklin arrives in Philadelphia at age 17.
1731	Franklin founds the Library Company of Philadelphia.
1744	Franklin founds the first fire insurance company in America.
1751	Liberty Bell is ordered from London.
1753	Pennsylvania State House (Independence Hall) is built.
1774	Carpenter's Hall is completed. First Continental Congress meets there.
1775	George Washington is appointed commander in chief in Independence Hall. Continental Congress elects Benjamin Franklin the first Postmaster General of the United Colonies.
1776	Declaration of Independence is written in Independence Hall.
1777	The British enter Philadelphia on September 26. More than 2,000 unknown soldiers of the Revolutionary War are buried in what will be called Washington Square.
1778	On June 18, the British evacuate Philadelphia.
1787	Constitution is written in Independence Hall.
1790	Ben Franklin dies on April 17.
1790–1800	Philadelphia is the capital of the United States.
1791	Old City Hall opens for governing Philadelphia. First Bank of the United States is chartered; it will be built at Third and Chestnut streets.
1793	Yellow Fever sweeps through Philadelphia, killing over 4,000 people. It will strike again in 1797, 1798, 1800, 1802. Congress passes the Fugitive Slave Act.
1797	Washington resigns; John Adams becomes second president.
1797–1798	Polish Revolutionary War hero Thaddeus Kosciuszko comes to Philadelphia and is visited by many American dignitaries.
1816	Second Bank of the United States is incorporated. It is famous for its classical Greek architecture.
1829	The cornerstone for the U.S. Mint at Chestnut and Juniper Streets is laid.
1838–1844	Edgar Allan Poe lives in Philly, where he writes "Murders at Rue Morgue" and "The Tell-Tale Heart."

1850	On July 9 the Great Fire, which started on Vine Street Wharf, destroys 367 houses.
1865	On January 28, the Delaware River freezes over; people walk over it to New Jersey.
1872	The iron steamship *Pennsylvania*, the first vessel of the American Steamship Company of Philadelphia, is launched at William Cramp and Sons' shipyard on Beach and Norris Streets.
1876	Philadelphia Museum of Art is established.
1883	Phillies baseball team is formed.
1926	Delaware River Bridge—now called the Ben Franklin Bridge—opens.
1930s	Pat and Henry Olivieri invent the cheese steak sandwich.
1946	ENIAC computer is built at Pennsylvania State University.
1952	*Bandstand*, later called *American Bandstand*, premieres; the Philly show would become a national sensation in 1957.
1960s	Philly Soul musical style invented.
1962	Wilt Chamberlain scores 100 points for the Philadelphia Warriors in a 169-147 victory over the New York Knicks.
1967	The Philadelphia 76ers win the NBA championship.
1974	Philadelphia Flyers hockey team wins the Stanley Cup.
1975	The Flyers win the Stanley Cup for the second year in a row. "Philadelphia Freedom," a song by Elton John, is a number one hit.
1978	The Phillie Phanatic becomes Philadelphia's Major League Baseball team's mascot.
1980	The Philadelphia Phillies win their first championship.
1985	Live AID concert is held at JFK Stadium to raise money to feed the world's hungry. The mayor of Philadelphia bombs a radical group called MOVE and sets the city on fire; 11 people die as a result.
1987	One Liberty Place is constructed; it is the first Philadelphia building allowed to be taller than City Hall.
2007	An archaeological dig unearths part of the president's house that was used from 1790 to 1800.
2008	Philadelphia Phillies baseball team wins the World Series for the second time in their history.
2009	President-elect Barack Obama and his vice president Joe Biden begin their historic train ride to the inauguration in Washington, D.C., at Philadelphia's Penn Station.

Further Reading

Books

Fleming, Thomas J. *Ben Franklin: Inventing America.* New York: Sterling Publications, 2007.

Gillis, Jennifer Blizin. *William Penn.* Chicago: Heinemann Library, 2005.

Landau, Elaine. *Independence Day: Birthday of the United States.* Berkeley Heights, New Jersey: Enslow Publishers, 2001.

McDonald, Megan, *Saving the Liberty Bell.* New York: Atheneum Books for Young Readers, 2005.

Randolph, Ryan P. *Betsy Ross: The American Flag and Life in a Young America.* New York: PowerPlus Books, 2002.

Internet Sources

The City of Philadelphia, Official Site
http://www.phila.gov

Franklin Institute
http://www2.fi.edu/

Independence Hall
http://www.nps.gov/inde

Independence National Historical Park
http://www.nps.gov/inde/

National Constitution Center
http://constitutioncenter.org/

Philadelphia Convention and Visitor's Bureau
http://www.philadelphiausa.travel/

Works Consulted

Donohue, Amy. *Frommer's Philadelphia & the Amish Country*. Hoboken, New Jersey: Wiley Publishing, Inc., 2005.

Mobil Travel Guide—Mid-Atlantic. Lincolnwood, Illinois, Publications International, Ltd., 2007.

Philadelphia & the Pennsylvania Dutch Country. New York: Fodor's Travel, Random House, Inc, 2008.

Smith, Jane Ockershausen. *The Philadelphia One-Day Trip Book*. McLean, Virginia: EPM Publications, Inc., 1985.

Weigley, Russell F. (editor). *Philadelphia: A 300-Year History*. New York: W.W. Norton & Company, 1982.

Wilson, George. *Yesterday's Philadelphia*. Miami, Florida: E.A. Seemann Publishing, Inc., 1975.

President-elect Barack Obama leaving Penn Station in Philadelphia

Glossary

anthropologist (an-throh-PAH-luh-jist)—Someone who studies how human beings have lived through time.

centennial (sen-TEH-nee-ul)—The 100-year mark.

delegate (DEH-leh-git)—A person who represents a group of people.

inspire (in-SPYR)—To excite (someone) to action.

landscape (LAND-skayp)—Plant and design and area according to a plan.

orchard (OR-churd)—An area of fruit trees or nut trees planted for harvest.

pamphlet (PAM-flet)—A short unbound publication.

reenactor (ree-en-AK-tor)—A person who dresses and acts as if he or she is living in an historic time period.

revitalize (ree-VEYE-tuh-lyz)—To bring new life to.

sensation (sen-SAY-shun)—Excitement.

textile (TEX-tyl)—Woven fabric; yarn or thread used to make cloth.

Index

ABOUT THE AUTHOR

Russell Roberts has written and published nearly 40 books for adults and children on a variety of subjects, including baseball, memory power, business, New Jersey history, and travel. He has written numerous books for Mitchell Lane Publishers, including *Holidays and Celebrations in Colonial America, What's So Great About Daniel Boone, Poseidon, The Life and Times of Nostradamus,* and *The Lost Continent of Atlantis.* He has lived in Bordentown, New Jersey—just across the river from Philadelphia—for many years.